SPONTANé

COLLECTION OF SELECTED RECOLLECTIONS

QALANDAR_AM

To the Great Thenkurissi Sankara Menon,

Traveller, Humanitarian & Grandfather

The hug that I longed...

The cuddle that I missed!

Contents

Contents

Foreword

Dear Reader,

I asked many to write a foreword for the poems, since they were moving in fast forward, they couldn't manage to. Many read my manuscript but couldn't write on it. So I keep this page for my readers. As Walt Whitman said;

"For song, issuing from its birth-place, after fulfilment, wandering,

Reck'd or unreck'd, duly with love returns."

Come back to me once you read. I will be here only without moving 'Forward'.

Qalandar_am

Preface

Perhaps, Reader, this preface may be the tethys where all the amazons of thought I have towards the world merge. The sea change from a boy who loved only Coke Studio, movies, his Tata Nano and some Eau de Parfums, to a thirty four year old baby, who now silent at everything is pretty remarkable. The world believed that finally I got adapted. Actually, I trapped the world to believe that. Fortunately I am still with James Baldwin, who gave the questioning everything and pulverising theory. Outside I am that bald who never won because the world wants to see me like that. Inside I am that wanderer, that qalandar who smells of vetiver and agarwood. Always fresh and ready for the journey which the mundane calls as risks. I am in a process to elevate myself into the status of KAVI, the all knowing, the all explaining, ultimately the all journeying, KAVI. Poetry is creation, a godly activity. Since the Ubermensch made us in his form, I strictly believe he has given his powers too. We are all creators. Some recreate, some procreate, some miscreate. Creation of some sort will always prevail in this world. I am the amalgamation of re, pro, and mis, so is my poetry. Let's read...

I have only one request to my readers, read as you like and explain as you can. My thoughts are just fragments. Wandering and going through a multitude of situations. May be my soul bin has or had better poems. Sometimes I have a revisit. Out of those, I selected only those which I felt better. This may be your worse or best, but once you got hold of this collection, please read at least once, may be it will take you somewhere or to someone.

Dear Readers!

We are all like books.

We have an author,

We have a publisher,

And of course, we have a reader.

Read or unread we will be,

But will always be reprinted,

If the content is GOOD!

Acknowledgements

Time... for being patient enough to wait for me...
Starting from the classics to the moderns, all those poets who
observed whatever I wrote and gave apt suggestions during my
pursuits...
My Muse...For being with me everytime...
My Mom... for that hot black tea during my nocturnal
draftings...
Dad... for believing in me... always...
My Uncle... for analysing and giving me the right direction...
Mema and Mama... ever positive and ever supportive...
My Brother... for those wonderful emojies after reading my
works...
My Friend... for those positive exclamtions, everytime...
Finally and most importanlty,
Calicut and Khordha...
For those sangria evenings of light and delight... with a hint of
Masala Chai...

Prologue

I am myself the 'prologuer' and 'foreworder'. Nothing to say to you all. I am already dead and from my death, the readers begin. Happy reading... See you at the epilogue.

1. Overture

I
Walked
With burden
Of loneliness.
Suddenly the wind
Came by and enquired this
Poet's sadness and took me
Near the creek where the trees stood tall
The wind trumpeted, "Mates! Meet my mate
From le monde des mortels. He includes both
Of us; stuck like you with a soul like me.

2. The Masquerade – A Reverie

I was also invited,

To the masque of uninvited.

The innkeeper prayed not to go

Curious was I and went unmasked,

To my wonder, there were no masks.

The faces changed as I turned away,

Pink to red, then black and grey.

Wrinkles come and go,

Teeth to fangs and nails to claws grow!

There was a little red riding hood,

And a malicious Mr. Big Bad Wolf.

I heard the tiger's roar of ecstasy,

When it heard the wailing of a lamb in agony.

But the hyena was quick with its staccato,

The vulture roosting on the chandelier,

Spread its wings as gratitude.

I ran to the lamb

Set it free.

It looked to my eye

"you ruined my game"

It gave a howl

I saw its fangs…

Three little pigs,

Squeaked mockingly,

I was cornered.

All the men and all the women,

Charged against me

"Remove your mask, what are you?"

A faceless one came with a dagger

I lost my face.

He smiled "now we are one!"

Without eyelids, I looked at them

Through them arrived a beautiful lady

She looked at me, asked "dear knight,

Shall we play a game of chess?"

My lipless lips tapped together "who are you beautiful?"

She smiled "a dame sans merci"

Her laugh was contagious

All my horses and all my knights perished in the battle

I looked at those perfect white and black squares

Black contains the blood

White contains the bones

A long shadow of a scythe was filling me

I looked upwards to find a grey cloak of infinite vastness

Looking at me with its hollow face

Yelled, "You have finished your race!"

The masque is finished

So was I

Two coins I placed on my eyes

Heard the rows
Charon took me up
I moved through the men
Through the laughs
Through the caverns and corridors
Through the battlefields
Through the valleys wild
Beyond beyond as the rows muttered
Waiting I lay… for the next masquerade…
19/03/2020

3. Conversation with a Hangman

It is meticulous

Pure art it is

I elevate into a trance Saheb!

Nasha! We call it Nasha.

They are brought…

Their black heads are already hanging

Guilt? One police saheb asked,

No! They can't bear the sight of that

That's the reason. The other one muttered!

The overture…

They are placed under the beam

Like ascending notes

Happily but slowly I tie their legs

They are cold,

As if I am tying a dead body.

Then to the neck.

Ahhh! The crescendo

The Garland finds its comfort

It likes the pumping

You should see saheb!

It trembles a little

As the roads inside that black head

Bumpy and narrow…

Life travels through it.

I was like a wind,

Eloquent but swift

Tak tak tak…

I am near the lever

Silence…

I looked my sahebs

Their red eyes are on my face

Waiting for it to green itself

I felt the inhale of the black heads

They have nothing to exhale

It's green…

The lever shrieked

The notes descended

And snapped

Suspended!

Their big toes tried to touch the ground

Of course they are not ballerinas

Failed miserably…

It was a purgation saheb!

I smiled for my success

Fellow hangmen say I am mad

I am happy for killing…

Bollocks Saheb! Sheer Bollocks!

Who likes to kill?

But it is my job

Luckily not my routine,
We are an endangered species…
I hanged four today
When will be the next… don't know,
Red tapes should be tight,
Then only white ropes will emerge.
With this the hangman smiled and smoked his Pipe.
I looked at him as the smoke surrounded his neck.
He hanged his head…
I too heard the snap.
20/03/2020

4. A Confrontation

He started weaving at the top corner

He felt it was good

And rested on the seventh day

He saw me as his ADAM

Oh, that looks!

Eight glass marbles

Arranged on the top

Of the Whitman[1] beard

Two fangs

Eight legs

Eight directions

He was everywhere

The hairy PAGAN

Easily decoding my movements

I can't perform my sins

The glass marbles

Always had my image

Imprinted

It moved to hunt

But his eyes were on me

I was his bigger prey

The web was getting bigger

Its network flourished

He can reach me now

I made my mind

I will instill

The seven plagues [2] upon it

I am Forgetting

What my Sultan [3] said!

I took my civilized broom

Looked for the opportunity

He was absent that day

I like a fallen Angel

Charged with all my rage

Destroyed his silky heaven

Then he arrived

He looked at me

From the mid-air

His hands were spread

As if he was going

To perform a miracle

I didn't think twice

I thrust my spear

He looked at me

He was Jesus

And I, the centurion

Longinus [4]

He lost from my sight

Or was I became blind?

I slept in peace.

The third day I saw him
Emerging towards
The corner
He has risen
He calmly looked at me
Eight glass marbles
Arranged on the top
Of the Whitman beard
Two fangs
Eight legs
Eight directions
I rubbed my eyes
He moved his jaws
What was he muttering?
Because you have seen me,
You have believed [5]
I looked for my weapons
But the light blinded me
I couldn't look upwards.
Through the light,
His shadow surrounded
Engulfed the room
Penetrated my heart
Caught my brains
The Rest is silence [6]
21/03/2020

5. Aananda Thandav - The Dance of Joy

I

The Red Giant spilled crimson and amber

Shukra[1] with his pink palette,

Etched the clouds with Pink and Lavender

Himavan[2] looked up for the sight,

And the pink drops splattered on his visage.

He smiled and took a handful of water,

From Gangotri[3] and diffused with his white.

His hand touched the ripples,

Of Bhagirathi[4] and she took forward,

The colour of love from her pater,

Through the pebbles, chasms, corridors,

Into the valleys of Deodar, Birch and Fir.

The mossy duns[5] roared the smell of woody incense,

The Ringals[6] sang Durga[7],

The wind came touching all,

And ascended high with the incense and song

He cleansed himself with the drizzles of Indra[8],

Elevated high caressing the divine lotuses

II

Himavan smelled the Raga,

And listened to the incense.

Splendid was Durga's high notes,

Embalmed the air with warmth of joy.

Like the top notes of citrus,

Adorning the redolence.

The middle notes of lavender pink,

Swam across the lotus pond,

And evaporated towards the sky,

The essence of balance.

In the heart, it was cedar, sandal and amber.

The divinity of the dusk reverberated through,

The mantra of Durga and burst out,

Into a thousand vibrant immutable[9],

As it slowly touches the pellet drum,

Placed high on the wisdom atmosphere.

Hearing the call, the Eternal awakes…

III

The Poet caressed his setting,

Eight directions and three worlds.

The Muse* sat beside him,

They bathed in the Colour of Love

The Moon mixed the hue of blue,

Put tiny sparkles in the sky.

And descended towards him.

Crescent, he became and,

Sat beside our Timeless.

Still as a connoisseur,

Waiting for the moves.

The Ophidian loosens his grip,
From the Lord of the Beasts.
The benign poet always dances,
Beyond the endless coils.
The trident shined in the twilight
He took the pellet drum,
It emitted the radiance of the
Transcendental signified.
He thought for a moment,
"Beyond the bondages of
Knowing and unknowing
Far away from the senses
And the heinous consciousness,
Attached and detached,
I was born
Or was I unborn?
Not my concern.
I am nameless
But in every name,
I rest.
What am I?
In this vast multiverse,
Of endless creation and destruction?
Just a vessel!
An Eternal Kapaala[10],
Filled and emptied…"
The conch roared "it is time"

"I am perpetual knowing,

And Bliss…

I am Shiva

Beyond the binaries,

Betwixt the unities.

I am source,

And its pursuit"

With this the Ceaseless,

Stepped his right foot,

Squeezing the spiritual Ignorance,

He swirled his trident.

His army accompanied his moments

The Three worlds joined

The Dance of Joy overflowed

Creation rejoiced

The third eye[11] unfurled…

29/03/2020

6. The Crown

The kingdom devoid of sun,
The netherworld.
Looking to the sub lunar,
The Knight said to the Crown!
"Our Travel accounts, Sire
With the ballads of their conquest
Filled with maps
Latitudes and longitudes
They boasted
"How quick we were?"
The visit was small
But it was imperial
Like rivers merged with the sea,
We merged with them
The Byzantine,
The land of the brainy!
Ha… still gets me,
With their philosophies,
Tongue twisters to us
Hard to say
Easy to forget
But always quarrelsome
They differ and defer,

Easy for us to infer,

They are sure to suffer.

That entire Old world,

Now missing those beautiful steppes.

Ah… the Venetians,

Boastful but calm,

Pretentious and chaotic

Easiest they were to claim.

The empire where the sun never sets,

The hardest to crack

Yet we won!

Magnificent Marseille[1]

Strong Le Mistral[2], that le vieux port[3]

Which welcomed us as her lover.

Finally the third…

Rats simply rats Sire…

Running hith and thith[4]

Their poverty was infamous

Their resistances were famous

Poor chaps…

Swamps of degenerates,

They Lie Terror stricken

Between the headless Crowns

After the wars we missed the mark

Development – The New World!

We receded from many.

We still have some,

In the third and the dark.

Not good sire…

Our Empire should grow

The crown should be vast

But they are connected now…

Believing they are uncolonized!"

For this the Crown Smiled

Calmly he proclaimed,

"Connection is the key!

We will join them…

Let's spread

Among them

As them

For them

By Them.

Colonization of some sort should go on

They will try to break it

But fear not,

The crown is always with you My Knight!

Let's March from the East…"

07/04/2020

7. Khyber

The citadel[2] got decayed,
By the showers absurd.
Sindhu lies still, lost,
Her vigour and shimmer.
The civilization sapped out,
Of its vitality stood for mercy.
The Mountains looked her,
The corridor asked,
"What ails you Sindhu?
The enquiry echoed.
With a sullen face,
The River rippled
"My dear fort!
I know not…
A stillness invades,
Decaying subjects,
Detouring course
My sister[3] just evanesced!
Ghost she became.
Her subjects wandered
Not a trace Yet…
Boundaries emerged
Spears were made,

Checked its points,
Piercing other's flesh.
Yes! They were sharp.
Lepers and wretched Palsies
Fed on me and I took,
Their itching pestilence.
They put stones on me,
Diverged me from them,
And now they are craving.
Mound of dead it is now.
Crackling of bones I hear,
From those citadels of fear.
Lapis Lazuli squirts blood,
Priests chant nonsense,
No dance and no games.
Masters of River They claim!
Ha! Nincompoops…
Their false - gold weapons,
Now black as their iris
Lost its shine…
Their skinny shape,
Like twigs of an old fir.
They are dying.
They need to be leaving.
But where I don't know.
Oblige me my eternal elder!
(Hearing this plea,

The great passage

Soothed his sister

With a smooth wind)

"Dear perennial,

Fear not…

This great Passage,

Has seen enough.

Protected they were,

Lulled by thy ripples.

Subjects of decay,

They are, alas!

Imminent, their passage.

The boastful Janus[4] – minded!

Looks to the past and future,

Deteriorates his self in present.

Doubtful about himself,

Ends in chaos,

Like flies to fire.

An untimely demise!

Civilian and civilization,

Transitions and transgressions.

Human it is… My dear!

You flow and I give passage.

Their life is somewhere.

Eternally deferred,

Their destination is.

Just carry them,

Till they spit on you
Till they cover me
Till they dissolve,
Among us."
Sindhu smiled,
As reassured.
"Some Pastorals[5] Await
Shall I send them?"
Enquired the passage.
"Let them be nurtured,
For they too tend to decay.
Let us wait…
I see an expansion,
Of the two legged shadow.
Spitting boring couplets,
Of their puny heroics.
Usual passages through us,
But more scrolls to his stories.
Let THAT boast as a conqueror,
And drive away the others.
Only to be driven by some OTHER."
With that, the Passage opened.
The river saw two legged ones.
Ravening creatures ran to her,
And sucked the Adam's ale[6].
The great corridor laughed,
"Fear not my dear Perennial,

THESE TOO SHALL PASS!"
09/04/2020

8. Countenances

I was sauntering at Ghent[1],
The day succeeding the LENT[2].
Came across the Old Masters,
Filled with exquisite expertise.
Struck with this near rectangled,
Eloquent canvas of faces entangled.
Christus draagt het kruis[3], it writ.
My mind muttered Jheronimus[4]…
The curator uttered Anonymous.
Her visage experimente[5] attacked,
My educated countenance defended.
Defeated, I turned to the others,
They were more vicious.
The Impenitent[6] was hissing,
Like Joe Blake[7] towards viverrines[8].
The Penitent[9] was stoned by the
Spittle of the nobles ignoble.
His cries sank in the murk,
Of sweat, blood and sunlight.
One has arrived to wipe a face[10],
And blessed with an imprint,
Stained in blood and flesh.
It is certain she will cherish.

The cavalcade taps their toes,

To the heartbeat of carnival.

Pompous legion celebrate.

Horses neigh for the Empire,

And Holy of Holies[11].

Ah! Hidden among them,

I see a lineament haggard[12].

Carrying the weight,

To the shiny bald head[13].

Betwixt this carnivalesque,

Hodgepodge, staggered the Son,

Tranquil towards the Empyrean[14]

Via Dolorosa[15] with thorn and Pelt[16].

"Over there THE MAN OF SORROWS[17],

Is exhibited". A voice emerged.

The curator left for the others.

SON of MAN who lived for others.

Brooding, I stood there still.

10/04/2020

9. Safeer – The Man Eater of Nagarhole

Red was the waters of Sigur[3] yesterday.

The stripes of terror withered away.

I heard the white's shot miles away.

My brother lived his last yesterday.

Now a rug that fits a Gossain's[4] rear,

Or stuffed, looking at Anderson's[5] gear.

Memorialized as Blue Mountain's[6] fear.

Rest in silence and save a seat for me,

As vengeance grows like a bush fire,

Its scorching heat is raging in me.

For you brother, I'll double my mane,

And unleash in Nagarhole as real bane.

Last kill was that skinny male white,

Who chanted, 'Tyger Tyger, burning bright.'[7]

Devoured got the verse along with his flesh.

Not bidding farewell from my papillae[8],

Flows down when it touches the prey,

It yells with fear, 'Ahhh! Tyger Tyger!'

Joy to ears that cacophony of fear.

My roar whirls through the santalums[9],

Create ripples of unrest in the kabini[10].

Fools, better build up your snares,

For I'll unleash as the ten plagues[11].
Awaiting you all at the Ground Royale,
As I heard two of them are from Ullal[12],
Dear to the Lords and Fakirs they are.
Let them arrive and show what they are,
For I am SAFEER, Terror of Nagarhole.
Mediator I am between Man and Morte.
The light of the lunar is still away,
Ravenous I am and crouching I lay.
Get a nice juicy lamb, an entrée I say.
Wave your torches you may get deceived,
The woods hide me you won't see my hide.
Be silent, the Nocturnals may cheat you,
For the nature am I and is against you.
If you found two shining dots of mockery,
Do fear, tis the tip of that 'Fearful Symmetry [13].'
10/04/2020

10. Rudra Thandav - The Dance of Destruction

Rudra Thandav - The Dance of Destruction

The scent of ash spreads Spiritus Mundi[1].

Ashen wind enwrapped the blackened sky,

Blotted out the stars with its greyish dye.

It is darkness! Dark as darkness should be.

Notes of sadness the mighty rivers echoed,

Turbulence reverberated in his divine abode.

Everything is ash now, the unassailable Ash.

He took a handful, and caressed it. "Alas,

A feeble amount of warmth in it.

The warmth of a life incomplete."

Emitting the rage, his third eye unfurled.

"Vanished is now what completed me,

Neither SI I am nor am I VA[2]. Lies in me,

Only the fire of apocalypse. It will burn,

Fanned by the cosmic winds. Will unleash,

Upon everything followed by the Thunder,

Destroys to nurture, for it has compassion,

Gives by annihilating evil, for it has control.

Empty my Eternal Kapala[3] is.

Refill time it is.

Uncleansed should be the cleansed.

Retained should be the balance

Complete should be the cycle.

HEAR HEAR HEAR! I am RUDRA!

The destroyer and preserver

Let this dance destroy,

Construction to construct

What is destroyed!

HERE HERE HERE! It is HERE!

The moment of truth is here,

Destruction shall be rejoiced."

Echoed his roar among the Tres Mundos[4],

Shattered with his rage was the dark clouds.

Ophidian uncoiled, untangled was his locks,

Danced with the Ganges and with the winds.

Ready for the task were his army and beasts.

The frenzy started and swirled the trident.

Whirled the world at his arrival imminent.

Chaos rejoiced and afraid was the ignorance.

The army descended for that reconnaissance.

He danced, they clashed, and wisdom triumphed.

The modus is perfect and result complete.

Life is that point where binaries compete,

Absolute confluence in diffluence absolute.

On the wisdom atmosphere he sat high,

Once again pacified with happiness high.

To his left the crescent bloomed high.

Shining was his trident and night was starry.

The three worlds flashed before his eyes.
Absolute beauty and feast for eyes,
He saw it was good and closed his eyes
The great poet among the trinity
Composed worlds in his vicinity.
15/04/2020

11. Ganges and the Grandsire

The twilight blew hard its conch of peace,
From ground, Red spread to the sky of peace.
Men and chariots a thousand slain today.
Betwixt them the white clad made his way,
Towards his dear mother in utter dismay.
The river of life stood in front of him,
Perennial, pure, white and ever youthful,
Her son, old, wise, white and ever woeful.
Smiles exchanged, caressing was heavenly,
Tears rolled out from the grandsire manly.
"What ails thee, O Grand patriarch of KURU?"
The son smiled and mother washed his tears.
"You come hither whenever your mind tears,
Tell me dear, what aches thee, o wise KURU?"
Reverted the mighty warrior with gloomy sigh,
"KURU, that royal stamp itself hurts me high,
Strived for its strength, protected its Lineage.
Loved its growth and pompous for its heritage,
Still that roll of dice it couldn't withstand,
And now on these rivulets of blood I stand.
Failed I am as a protector, but helpless I stand.
The boon, yes I received to control my demise

Made me kill my emotions and died many times,
Expecting something good may come as price.
Bed of arrows Ma! Without a pinch of solace,
Stop everything! I vouched against everyone,
Palace echoed my rage, but listened by none.
Like that Puru, I gave my youth to my pater.
Celibate, I transformed and helped to cater,
The grandest design of his dreams. I wonder,
The results were monstrous. Why? I ponder,
Did I do anything too bad for this kingdom?
Any fatal error unnoticed by my wisdom?
What's the use; here I am invaded by olddom.
In between, visions of her I see, The Princess,
Of Kashi and her pointed finger of vengeance!
Not afraid of it mother, and I have my excuse.
But like an albatross of sin, that debt remains.
Her view was correct but my vow was perfect.
In between us, crumbles this dynasty imperfect.
What happens in future determines the present,
I feel. My descent has gone into a steep descent."
Mother of life caressed him with sheer dissent.
"Introspective interrogation lends no vent!
Sure, crumbled was the lineage between the dice.
But to the kingship, love blindness is never wise,
The City of Elephants had flourished otherwise.
But elephants are elephants, a world of upheaval,
Driven by those mahouts, the seven sins primeval.

Dream of a heaven like the kingdom of lord Ram,
But charge against the other like a merciless ram.
Kuru, you are the doer. You executed duties well,
But it just echoed like voices in a waterless well.
Beacon you remain and have to lead them well,
You tried to refrain from war, but you know well,
Sides have to be taken in gambling, you took the right,
Now time has come to protect it with all the might."
The lady took her son's wrinkled hands. "The lines,
Mean a lot for me. The endeavor you took Shines,
Here and it will shine forever. Warrior's way it is!
Tomorrow, fight brave. Let your white shine bright.
Mother I am and always took my son's side. It is alright,
To take some rest after that. You have seen enough,
Controlled enough, hesitated and fought enough."
The grandsire bowed his head towards his mother.
Happily her fingers flowed through his white hair.
"Tomorrow will we meet ma?" "I am here my dear!
I have flowed before you, with you and flow after.
Tomorrow you sleep on my lap, lullabies will flow,
Into you. Hurdles are nil betwixt us tomorrow."
The son bid his farewell chanting tomorrow.
Happy he was for the future, finality was near.
The river saw him going, smiled "Finally he is near".
She removed every stone that obstructs her path,
Waited her son's comeback through that same path.
She muttered "tomorrow it is…"

The same echoed in the Grandsire's tent,

Tomorrow, that word became a lullaby.

Her promise put her child to sleep.

10/05/2020

This poem is a conversation between Bhishma and his mother

Ganga before his last war in kurukshetra against the Pandavas.

12. Heap of the Defile

The pebbles from Muzdalifah[1], I gathered
After the Maghrib[2] and Isha[3], rolled in my hands.
In front of me lies the heap of the defile,
And on it stands him, The Defiler smiling,
At me. "Pelt Him!" commanded the Malak[4],
Resting next to me. One I threw, the iblis
Laughed and showed my temptations.
The second I threw, he laughed more
And showed my crimes. When I threw,
The third it grew larger and touched,
The three worlds. "Distancing thou art,
From thy wishes, sacrificing thou art,
Thy needs in the name of that One."
"Throw the fourth, distanced he has to be"
The Malak commanded, I chanted,
The names of the Merciful and pelted,
The fourth showed my distressed life,
The fifth showed my escape from it.
An affluent mirror it transformed,
At the sixth. It showed nothing but I,
Smiling a devilish smile at myself.
"Throw the seventh, shatter thyself
From these illusions. Thou knowest,

Well that thy life is his blessing.

The all beneficent, The Most Merciful,

The Sovereign, the Holy Giver of Peace,

Security he grants, Absolutely he controls,

Exalted he is and omnipotent, Great Absolute,

Author. Eternal Spirit worshipped by all,

Artist He is and the Absolute Forgiver,

He is adorned by many beautiful names.

He knows us and protects us. Beware

Thy detours from him, for he is The,

Ultimate Witness. He is the outward,

Sign of the Inner Mysteries of us and

The Universe. Fear not the Defiler,

He is no Near the One who is Beyond

The Internal and Beyond the Outward

Before the Foremost and After the Final.

Understand! Thou art the vessel of Good

And also The Heap of The Defile.

Thou art the Pillar of Good and Evil.

Throw the stone towards thy mirror

The internal despot resides in thee,

Your Nafs[5] should be cleansed and

Distanced from Iblis[6]. Pelt towards thyself!

If Ibrahim[7] succeded thou shall … Pelt Son!"

The Great Malak Jibrail[8] thus flew away.

I threw the seventh to the mirror.

It shattered to a thousand and was gone.

The Smile collapsed and a clear silence,
Emerged inside enwrapped in the light
Of wisdom shined inside. The wind,
From the heavens blew the sign of freedom.
24/05/2020

13. Phobias

Two people met at bazaar
Repelled themselves.
Like poles they were.
But their phobias,
Got attracted.
They greeted.
The green got mixed
With the saffron one,
A pestilence yellow.
Emerged.
They saw it was good.
Red and Blue arrived
Mixed with yellow.
Flames it was!
It spread across,
Those repelling ones.
These four,
Sat around a table
Sipped their routine tea
O! It was hot.
Four blew together.
Different breaths,
Fanned the flames.

They enjoyed their tea.
Belched out their Samoosas.
"Ate enough for today
More will be served
Tomorrow morning."
Green opined finality
Yes nodded the Saffron
"Constipation still exists"
Patting the belly,
The blue expressed.
"O don't bother,
The Conference is ready,
Writing will be exact,
So reading it maketh it
Smoooooth."
Smiled the red.
Un - bazaaring the bazaar,
They parted saying dasvidaniya.
28/05/2020

14. Trishanku

Suspended they are
Upside down.
In the midst
No right no left
No up, no down,
Forwards or,
Backwards,
They can't move.
Heaven can't take them,
Nor the mundi.
But crux they are!
Care crafted in paper
Is plenty among them.
Take ages to understand
Comes with an expiry
So they throw
Before its use.
Left cries utopia,
Right cries Shambhala[2],
In the midst,
Hangs them!
Looking both sides,
None forming a side.

Cheated they are,
Distanced they are.
Poles failed them
They wander,
Like in the Limbo[3],
Unbaptized.
Known as Masses
Without any mass.
Even media took sides,
Chained deemed as liberals.
What about these suspended?
They became neutral,
And Neutrals became chained,
Crippled like a Slow Man[4].
Prospect of A Right Side[5],
Waned as if writ in water[6].
Life is kafkaesque[7]
Like Samsa or K[8].
Fully metamorphosed
But have to die like a hound[9].
Unaware of death's reason.
Eons of life, death and rebirth,
Man to dog and dog to man.
Mark its territory
Lives there.
First leaves the stench.
And then the body.

Runs behind truth,

Like dogs behind bone.

Gets a meal of falsehood,

Roasted or grilled,

Ultimately half baked,

But garnished well

Gobble up, vomit some,

And Rest till the next.

Now Truth is plenty

And beauty is lost.

Confused they are,

Without a centre.

Some said to play,

Others versified,

Their lament.

Some enquired.

Went backwards,

Clicking forward.

"What is this place?"

Enquired the suspended.

"Thrishanku it is…

Between Scylla and Charybdis[10]."

Reply came like a bell.

"What is our duty?"

Enquiry was swift.

But the answer was the swiftest

"Compromise!"

28/05/2020

15. Truth

Truth
Yes, not like that pineapple,
Which just gets when peeled.
It's like that hard coconut,
Fortified.
Herculean task it is.
Rip the husk first,
Then the shell,
Ah! The Solid Albumen.
Inside comes the truth
Be careful! It might explode.
06/06/2020

16. The Raven on the Street

It was the cables!
It drew black lines
Of terror in the sky
Move through them,
Untouched was a task.
I was an expert and flew
Well. This time I missed.
It was sparkles. Lights
Of agony scattered.
It was a sight for the
Clay – made. The dark
Angel has fallen.
Their eyes glowed at it.
I looked upwards.
They were bigger,
Was I in brobdingnag?
I stayed there unmoved.
Eyes wide open right,
Beaked I remained.
They passed drawing crosses,
And interjections of pity,
With their binoculars.

The four wheeled invention
Went through me.
I stayed unmoved
Nothing to be done.
Three more passed.
I stayed unmoved
But my beak opened wide.
Was I crying?
Don't know!
Upwards I saw the BAT,
Felt sorry for the nocturnal
At night the game is darker
You can't see the line and
They remain silent too.
Stretched his wings were,
Eyes wide open!
My blood became brown,
Then to my raven black.
My body as per my will
Will be given to the
Lesser creatures.
They will come in,
Eventually!
The last one to pass by
Was a poet, I know him
A **'poeish'** guy,
In search of his lost Lenore.

He looked at me.

He thought for a while.

I flew and sat at his shoulder,

We walked together.

From worse to verse.

I looked back towards myself

The lesser ones have started crawling.

18/06/2020

POEISH – looking like Edgar Allen Poe – an American poet.

17. Alamgir

Looking straight,
At the chandelier
With eyes wrinkled
Like a raisin.
Alamgir smiled
The twilight of wisdom
Pacified his eyes.
Incense spread the room,
The news of his end.
The Timurid[2] closed his eyes
He saw the Malak al – Maut[3,]
Arriving to embrace him.
"Is it the hard way?"
He asked. The Malak,
Replied "only the soul knows!"
Alamgir smiled,
"Let me dream for a moment then."
The Malak waited.
Alamgir dreamt.
Holding abba's hands,
He enters a room
He stays at the door
The king roars to the boy

"Enter Muhi – ud – Din[4]!"

The boy said "you believe everyone

And I am not a fool. I will guard you."

He distanced himself

Stayed safe

For the Takht – e – Taus[5].

The tusk of death,

Was broken by his lance

Bahadur[6] he was.

He scoffed the Shah

As Filthy connoisseur

Who build the silly mausoleum

Chained him

Distanced him

Pidargir[7] he was.

Killed the king's mirror,

Dara - the wealthy terror.

Shuja, the idiot elder,

Died as a hungry beggar.

Murad rests in Gwalior

Silent as a slithering traitor.

Alam played the game well

Splendid was his Coronation.

The Reviver of Religion,

Was an ornament to the throne[8]!

Music irritated him.

Paintings were licentious.

The Gharanas[9] crumbled,

Under his reign.

The entire hadiths[10] he read,

The lives of saints he professed,

The fatawa[11] he compiled,

The caps he knitted,

Asserted the Fiqh[12]

Uttar and daccan[13].

Green and Saffron[14]

The corridors bled

The forts and treaties

Battle of flags,

He ruled the board

He was alamgir.

Still he believed none

He distanced himself

Distance was contagious

Palace walls began their distance

Then it was Yamuna

The fields of ganges

Gave out dry winds

Drier than loo[15]

Separated him and people

Attracted them to hunger

As no solace got from Langar[16]

Rats ate the caps,[17]

Maps and subjects.

He pardoned the whites,
And they played their cricket.
Viziers warned the impending death
Of the empire that Tamerlane dreamt
Even Tamerlane cried
Rasti Rasti[18]
But our Mughal didn't heed
Surahs began to get musical
They sang in Raag deepak[19]
The waters of Yamuna failed
To satiate his burns
He wished to hear Malhar[20]
The throne would have danced
But No he can't
It was haram.
Octogenarian he was,
Rebellions and campaigns
Distanced our Zinda Pir,[21]
From the takht
Wrinkles distanced him,
From smile and sight.
But he made sure,
That he was alive.
The hawk left
Seeking its directions,
After the pyrrhic victories.
"Am I alamgir really?"

The bony badshah ghazi[22]
Introspected.
"Am I alamgir really?"
The question alarmed,
The raisins.
The Malak was waiting
Alamgir spread his hand
Azam* was there,
He held the twig – like,
Fingers of the great lineage
And it spoke
"I know not who I am,
Where I shall go,"
To this the Malak smiled
It continued,
"My years have gone
By profit less"
Azam looked sharp
"Yet I am Alamgir"
It laughed scoffing itself
"God has been in my heart,
Yet my darkened eyes have
Not recognized his light.
He was the Alamgir
And I just a Seizer
Like that Sikander[23]
And the great Qaiser.[24]

Now the skin is left."
The malak extended its hands
The Alamgir extended his…
They met
Alamgir enquired
"Will there be malhar?"
Malak was silent
"No… right?"
Alamgir sighed
"For the one who severed heads
And knitted caps,
For the one who took sword
And qalam[25] for quran
In one lifetime,
Ambivalent, his fate will be.
May the peace of God be upon you!"
Thus the Mighty Mughal
Finally distanced his body.
The wind blew bhatiyar[26]
Yamuna danced
And painted,
The receding moon
Azam came out
Of the shamiana
His eyes pointed to Dilli
The takht awaits…
21/06/2020

18. Eclipse

Beware!
The shadow of the third
Betwixt you and your
Confidante is always
Fatal!
A bit late only vision arrives
Darkness is swift within that.
Fear not!
Distance from its venom
Eloquent you come out!
Beyond the shadow
Lies the stream of light
Where swans of wisdom swim
And eclipse will be eclipsed.
21/06/2020

19. The Chalk Circle

The court of the new King is in session.
Two mothers and a suckling emerged
One mother held his right,
And the other his left
Argument began.
"That's my kid." One said,
"No, he is my kid." Reverted the other.
"His Father?" enquiries emerged,
Synchronized Automated motherly replies
"Sorry, the kid is a bastard."
"And he knew it from the womb itself
We too haven't seen his father.
He always comes at night."
The kid smiled at it.
Mumbled pathetic.
The King remarked,
"So two mothers and no father!"
"Should have been the other way Right?"
"The other way is usual, this one is unique, Sire."
The Minister commented.
"What did my Father do at these dark times?"
I can't recall Sire, it was ancient history.
"Then I should use my intelligence"

Yes, Sire! Now I remember, He did that!"

The Minister's modest reply was quick.

"Draw the Circle!" Commanded the King

"Yell not my Lord, your throne is shaky!"

The Minister advised his new King

The king smiled out his teeth in shame,

"Will you draw the circle please?"

"That's more like it, my lord"

The minister ran his bleak chalk on the floor

And a circle was born enough to hold a suckling

"Please place that thing inside."

The bulky peach sat inside the circle

"Pull him you both ladies"

Tug of war emerged,

The ladies were quick.

On the verge of getting ripped,

The Kid began to yell.

"Should have been the other way Right?"

"The other way is usual, this one is unique, Sire."

The Minister commented.

"What did my Father do at these dark times?"

I can't recall Sire, it was ancient history.

"Then I should use my intelligence"

Yes, Sire! Now I remember, He did that!"

The Minister's modest reply was in repeat mode.

"Put him down!" The King yelled

Supporting his throne.

The mothers placed the kid in the circle.
Poor thing was caressing his hands
Mumbling something,
Possibly swearing,
In a language unknown.
Eyes red like raspberries.
"Let him decide where to go!"
The two mothers now began to persuade,
The lad. He, looking at them both.
"Do I know you both?"
Enquiry shined like effervescence
On the brim of his eyes.
Four hands begged at his sides.
Bargains and prospects,
Showered at him.
Two Mothers were like roads,
Both the roads were taken.
But the kid took the road,
Not at all travelled by,
And that is going to make all the difference.
He took straight to the King.
Baffled, the King looked everyone
"Were you the man who went by the night Sire?"
The queen's wifey side whispered.
"What nonsense! This is not my kid."
The King disgusted silent.
"Well, The Chalk circle never lies!"

The queen asserted wifely.

The Kid began to yell.

The King turned to the minister

"Should have been the other way Right?"

"The other way is usual, this one is unique, Sire."

The Minister commented.

"What did my Father do at these dark times?"

I can't recall Sire, it was ancient history.

"Then I should use my intelligence"

The King proclaimed

"Childless I am,

And he fits as my heir.

Your Future King is here

Justice is always served here."

Everyone lauded the King's vision

The two mothers got a death sentence

For practicing witchcraft

Burnt at stake they will be.

The King turned to the minister

"How is my Judgment?"

"Yes, Sire! Just like your Father

Now I remember, He did this!"

The Minister's modest nod was accepted.

"Make that circle permanent."

Ordered the King

"Oh! No need Sire, we just need chalks

Circles will be made and why permanent?

They are already infinite.
13/10/2020

20. The Ox and the Moron

"Will you set me free after the field is ploughed?"
"First I asked this to the plough,
I didn't receive an answer,
Then I asked the rope,
But it got all the way tighter.
Then I asked my tail
Just to hear its twisted tale,
Through my spine till my forehead.
The tongue asked my hoofs
And got the taste of dirt.
I again asked the whip
And it showed your hand and,
Your hand showed your face.
Now tell me from where I can get my liberty?
You Moron!
More on and more on!
When your hunger will quench?"
(The two-legged moron stopped ploughing and answered)
"Three rib cages asked their tongues,
When our hunger will quench?
Their tongues showed me and my ribs.
I asked my ribs the same question

And they showed me the seeds.

The seeds showed the plough

And it showed the Whip

And the whip showed you.

Now tell my oxy, what this moron should do?

My freedom is in your thralldom.

Your shackle is invisibly visible

It ends at you and starts at me

But mine is clearly invisible

I don't know where it starts and its end.

I look back every time to see the unseen whip,

And it makes lashes

The invisible blood flows.

The salt in my sweat burns my skin,

But inside, the question burns more

When our hunger will quench?

Help this moron my dear oxy…"

The Ox said nothing

"Shall I whip you again?

Will you move?

I see invisible whips nearing at me now!"

"As you wish you moron!

I am your domesticated wild one

Whip till my back breaks,

My liberty will be at the butcher's axe."

The plough moved like a staff

And soil gave way like the sea divided by Mosses

The sweat of the moron and tears of ox mixed well

On the boundary, a scarecrow was standing staring.

"What are you looking at? Enquired the ox.

"Nay, I am the poet, I heard you both."

"So?" asked the moron.

"Sorry I am a fence sitter,

Can't help you both and won't help also

Your condition is worse,

And fit for a verse.

Let the whips roar as thunder

Let the sweat and tears reach the heavens,

And come back as rain

Let brown give way to green

You can rest after that.

That time the crows will come

And I will scare them away

Hunger will be satiated

Liberty will be found

No feeling is final Gentlemen!"

17/10/2020

21. Kabulnama – History of Kabul in Haikus

"I have flown beyond,
Those mountains and valleys wild."
The kite broken sighed.

The pomegranates
Awaited stones from kids, but
Stones went somewhere else.

Stallions neighed restless,
In their stable with hopes of
A new Buzkashi.

The Bazaars vacant,
Sold Kohls, Henneh and Ittar once
Awaits arrival.

Now the city sleeps
Inhaling the poppies and
Is invisible.

Historic city,
Majestic and a witness
To a million lives.

Wars fought and Regimes
Crashed for the supremacy
Derelict it was.

Brits, Czars and Yankees

Came. Lines made the lives divided
Vitality lost.

The Valley now speak
Gunshots, rapes, and politics.
The Mountains echoed.

The land of horsemen
Corrupted by religion,
Law and alliance.

The land of horsemen
Now awaits the clear air and,
Music it forgot.

With his old suroz.
"ji ji ji ji ba ta ra"
(May you live long, live long long)
A musician sings

Kabul river and
Koh – i – Baba await the
Arrival of Spring.
Written when Kabul was invaded... again

22. Kites of Kabul

When the Pamir blew the cold winds,
My Nose[1] thumped up for a flight.
Cutting through the flocks of clouds,
Once I flew like a shepherd.
Light radiated and delight spread.
I was free to fly as my Yaar[2] ,
Had the string and control.
It was not bondage, but belief,
That he will never cut the Tar[3].
He cheered at my flight.
His eyes flew with me
We fought together.
I cut the tars of his rivals
And his Confidante ran
For the fallen ones.
I was his Tapoos[4] and preyed,
On other Kaghazba'd[5].
I was his pride.
Now dust began to blew
On my tail and memories.
We caught in a sandstorm,
Of Ideologies.
The storm ended and every dune

Got different!
The Tar broke and we got displaced.
My spine is injured and I can't move.
The winds are scarce now.
Or are they scared to blow?
The valleys missed the cheers of joy,
And the Pomegranate missed the pelting.
The stones hit somewhere else now.
Where my Yaarwill be now?
Will he be playing with new One?
No he won't, I am sure.
He may be thinking of me,
In some alien country,
Where lances like buildings,
Are erected; stopping the wind,
And clouds to enter.
OR did he…?
Shukran Allah!
My journey will end soon.
When I drift off,
Wearing the blanket of weariness,
I will wake up in a new valley.
I will meet you there.
Make me fly high my Yaar!
Your Tapoos will cut your contenders.
Your confidante will run to fetch them,
Across the barriers.

We will win once again!
10/04/2021

23. The Rat and the Quill
For William Shakespeare

His quill became a Speare

Pierced the heart of Inkwell

Took all his black blood

The blood dripped

A perfect Shake He did

And placed it on the white

The white absorbed it

And spread across every Sphere,

Like blood the Ambitious hands,

Wield after that murder.

It recorded all the foul deeds risen,

The marriage, Dirge and Prison.

Prophecies, Magic, Love,

And the silence heard six feet under

It left nothing even the nothingness.

It measured the fathoms of mind

Played with the phantoms of brain

The Sound, the Fury, the Thunder

The roar of the ravenous hounds,

Snares as small as a kerchief

And as sharp as rapier envenomed

It mocked the Mortals

Fools! It called them

Even the devils envied

intelligentia mortale,

Ascended towards the Sphere

Making the hell empty

The Puns made them Shake,

With laughter.

Shaken,

Were they with maladies cathartic,

But enwrapped,

Were they in melodies iambic.

The quill worked its magic.

Words and words it poured,

Into the sea of the Saxons

Fools mocked it,

For knowing Little and Less,

The language of the Antiquus.

But it grew.

It invented in times of necessity,

Metamorphosed the existing.

Still wielder of the Quill,

THE RAT he was called.

AH! Modern Rodents!

Dissected him,

Left and Right,

Up and Down.

Only to say,

He is not of an age,
But for all time.
Some mocked him Thief.
Said he stole the Quill,
And killed the bearer,
With his sharp Speare.
The humble Swan of Avon
Replied Even Before this Question
With another question
What's in a Name?
So sure He was
Even before Saussure
The Quill now rests.
He who wielded it too,
Rests With ANNE,
Who HATH those Lips
That altered "I Hate".
AWAY she threw the HATE,
And saved his life, saying "not you."
23/04/2021

24. Dosai (Crepe)

The phone struck five,
She switched on herself.
'Active Mode' says she.
Granny smiles at her,
Phototropism!
Towards Granny she leans,
Picks her up,
Cleans her,
Oil,
Powder,
Cream,
Dresses,
She perfects her.
Granny smiles at her.
Round white countenance.
"What's for breakfast?"
"Dosai!"
The phone struck six
She accelerated herself
'Hyper Mode' says she.
Dad arrives after routine.
Peaceful!
As magic, the paper arrives

Flying to his hands
He peeps into the kitchen.
'Ehhhh…Tea?'
Tea arrives,
As train arrives,
From nilgiris.
Dad ate the news,
Drank the tea,
Belched out politics.
"What's for breakfast?"
"Dosai!"
The phone struck Seven
Mode and Mood,
Undecipherable.
My turn
"Breakfast?"
Brevity at its best
Smile was the answer.
My face sizzled.
Witnessed the genesis.
As if in a spell,
The ladle swims,
Silently,
With her help,
And comes up,
With a dollop,
Of batter.

It slowly glides,
Towards the pan,
A dollop falls,
The Pan Rejoices,
The ladle skates,
With her help.
Air escapes,
Dosai shines,
Like a Freckled moon,
In some dark night
Into that she
Drops butter.
Like gold in snow.
It shines!
I melted!
The dosai met,
With chutney.
Perfect confluence
"Motherly"
My mind explained
"Heavenly"
Opined her Man.
"Good but spicy"
Opined her mom.
"Three more dosai
After that I will eat."
She calculated herself

Finally she sat to eat.
A question emerged,
From somewhere.
"What's for lunch?"
It was the phone,
And it struck nine.
Written on a Mothers Day

25. Chottu – The Little One

Yesterday visited a Dhaba
Not posh but, decent it was
Waiter came and stood
With a crescent on his face
I ordered a clean table first
"Right away saheb" he rushed
From inside came rushing,
A five and half foot body,
With towel and liquid,
For cleaning the table.
I couldn't see his face.
The towel and tray covered,
Like dark clouds covered the sun.
Son of some mother somewhere,
Did his job perfect and scanned.
He passed a smile towards me,
Stating, "Is it clean Saheb?
Or do I need to clean more?"
Doubtful smile waited for me.
"Chottu!" the call from inside,
Awakened him from his doubt.
There is no table for doubt!

He rushed to the next one.

Water came, plates came,

Starters came,

Knives and forks attacked,

The plates and meat.

Their shrieks reverberated,

The walls. Belches heard from

Here and there, Orgasmic!

Chottu stood witness to all these.

He came with a trolley,

Gently took away the causalities.

Cleared the battlefield for the next.

I was at the cash, a space filled with,

Incense, Vermillion, Gods and Goddess.

In between sat a fat person cleaning,

The board stating "No Credit".

I Paid and asked "That boy?"

He smiled "AH, Chottu he is,

Did he trouble you?"

"No!" I said "But…"

Something caught my tongue

Fennel it was, May be.

The man laughed and said,

"You can find Chottus everywhere.

In hotels, quarries, factories,

They are proud breadwinners."

I took a twenty rupee note and said

"I would like to give him this…"
The man grabbed it "Thank you,
I will give it to him. So kind of you!"
Felt like Goddess of Wealth grinned.
Was she scoffing or giving consent?
I couldn't calculate.
I bid farewell and started wheeling.
Chottu might be continuing with a smile.
That night I thought of him.
He might have returned to his home.
His mom might be there waiting.
He gave her some money,
"Usual MA! And a ten rupee as tip."
I suddenly got up and heard
The smile of the Mother,
The smile of Chottu,
The Laugh of the Cashier,
And lastly,
The grin of the Goddess of Wealth.
She was scoffing indeed.
12/06/2021

26. Ubermensch

The Ubermensch came back
Sweat oozed down from him
Attire was soggy and bloody
He removed the protections,
Caressed the battle wounds
Sat on the crater in the couch
Reserved for him. Sighed!
The remote spoke the channels
It spoke of a cookery show
He smiled at it and watched
His better half gave him tea.
Sipped it but it didn't quench
His thirst from the battles
He fought, won and lost.
"How was your day?" she asked
"Just like your question." He
Smiled. He stationed his eyes
At the cookery show. "Voila!
That is a perfect Bolognese."
Searched pen to write the recipe.
Got from the sac en cuir and
Started to write. Oh! Not enough
Needs his other pair of eyes.

An Ubermensch needs four eyes
To look normal.
He cooked the dish in paper.
Finished!
He stood up, stretched and cracked
The air between his bones and joints.
Sighed he looked downwards
Hot tub was ready. He dipped himself.
The water absorbed the dirt
He scrubbed and wiped the day's labour
And felt relaxed at the hot water.
He got off and took his night pants.
The side kick ran towards him.
Happy he was as his idol came
And shared his heroics.
Suddenly the alert button beeped
The monster attacked the town
'Wrath of a Super Monster'
Sidekick took his tools
They both reached the city
Buildings have destroyed
Cars and figures are scattered
Grrr! Raaa! Roarrrrr!
Barboteuse Monstre roared wild
With the little mouth
That just finished its milk.
Ubremensch was to rescue

"Kick it Uber! Kick it."

He kicked it. Kick was feeble

But the monster bounced

Through that butterfingers and

Flew into the sea petrified.

The side kick was happy.

So were the people.

City played the hero's music

The Mayor gave him a shield

The Sidekick got his skittles.

Ate his reward and burped

They received a call

Headquarters it was

The Ubermensch took the sidekick

Breaking the sonic barrier

He flew through the night sky

They reached their cave.

Discussed about tomorrow's task

And gave a good night.

The guardian smiled in pride.

Switched off the lights,

Along with his smile.

He sat on his alpha chair

Cloak of reality invaded him

And introspected on the alien realm

His source.

He was like that Faustus

Who sold his soul.
The deviant comes to claim it
Every day.
He was a refugee there
Targets, crookedness, politics
Not his way and will not be.
He missed what he was and moved on
With his routine passed on to him
By the previous refugees.
Going back is not an option for him.
Eternal immigrant he will be.
Bread winners discovered fire,
They created wheel, they wandered,
Migrated, fought, they won and lost
In other Earths and Moons
To make their World a better place.
What was his dream?
He forgot as it was just a dream
He became many things
But not for himself.
He stopped thinking!
She called her to refuel
Dinner was good, he thanked Her.
Kissed his sidekick and prayed
Let him live his dreams one day.
He opened his Laptop,
Worked on his wars and targets

Deviants have shot messages
A new one opened.
"Sales low!"
Oh! A new monster has arrived.
Thought for a while
And typed the tactics.
Saved and posted.
Mail again
"You are saved for now.
Tomorrow a new task will be"
He reclined towards the chair.
The fan blew his sweaty hair heroically.
Heroic music intensifies somewhere.
And the side kick slept well,
Dreaming his Ubermensch
Battling imaginary dragons.
20/06/2021

27. Sultan - About Basheer

Beyond he was from his generation
Addicted towards life and progression
Stubborn he remained towards captivity
Humanist he scoffed at fool's felicity
Enchanted he was with Saigal[1] and Steens[2]
Elevated he was beyond barriers and screams
Rendezvous went well with the leveller today.
(The goat ate his pages
The inheritors too came
He happily scratched his back
And Saigal sang his part)
05/07/2021

28. Homecoming

Her eyes failed to bear the sight,
Yet looked from there with all her might.
Her home seemed dry and all cracked up,
"It was not like that when I went up!"
Introspected that delayed homecoming,
"Not yet! Not yet! It's unbecoming."
Some voice around commanded rude,
"Why I can't, please tell you crude.
She nurtured me to get till here,
And you control me to stay here.
I came to you on her consent,
Now I think she expects my descent.
Mother she is and you my father,
She can't bear my absence further.
Consent is what you have to give,
Return I shall if you fail to give."
Smiled the Pater on her ailment,
And sat near without discontent.
"Dear, your mother knows when to call.
But your siblings are behind her fall.
Sapped out her vitality and shimmer,
Burned her in the fires of summer.
Beaten and cracked up to the core,

Still, from her wounds they demand more.
They forget they are like alabaster,
Into her only they crumble faster.
Yet she won't summon you or me,
As it ruins our operandi.
We are to pardon them for eternity.
You are our pride and confluence,
And will surely return her affluence.
Let the time's chariot arrive for you,
Let your legion get ready for you.
They will position under my command,
Satiate your wish without any demand.
There will be elephants and cavalry,
Drums will herald your majestic entry.
Make mountains your step and descent,
To the valleys deep and rivers radiant.
They will give you way to your mother,
Cuddle she will but will not smother.
Heal her cracks with rivulets of love,
Verdant she will be by your act of love.
The mossy winds will take you to places,
Shower everywhere and shatter the mazes.
The ones who wait will be liberated,
Your homecoming will be celebrated."
10/07/2021

29. Window Shopping

Sold my eyes for the shades
Oh, that suit jacket! Loved it
Goes well with the Ivory shirt
For which I sold my hands,
Shoulders, spine, and stomach.
That ruby tie, expensive it is!
But will come for my neck.
AH! Those ebony trousers,
Made with the blackest black,
From the black hole, I think.
No light can pass through them.
Gravity is high, so sold the legs.
Feet went for the Oxfords and socks.
The wrist was reasonable for that,
Complex Tourbillon time machine.
My nose went to that Parfum vétiver,
Sniffed the green and bade au revoir.
My heart hurried to take a look,
At that rose gold Meisterstück.
Its clip gripped my patch pocket.
My lips were sold for one Cohiba,
And my head for that Cashmere hat.
The boutique was ready to close.

Still, I stood near that window.
Looking at the exhibits,
With a soul which I forgot.
It took a dissent,
And rested silent,
In the dark extent,
Of my wallet vacant.
11/07/2021

30. Lotus - eaters

Another day!
Weary, weary, and weary
Brushed tea with toothpaste
The toilet accepted my tittynopes.
Flushed out everything,
From Bingy and Brain.
The waters were alien to me.
Drops never embraced my body
It went straight down the abyss,
Of a common culture.
I remember the day,
I ate one lotus
And woke up to a dream
Where I flied on a Unicorn
Attacked the demons with smile.
The one eyed ones who saw only
The TARGET.
Pierced them with spears and won.
Distractions and deceptions.
Lured us like Sirens.
With wax, I closed my ears
And killed them too!
My cycles of hell should be

Finished I think

But Ithaca is FAR still.

We are Lotophages

It's been lot of ages.

Still intoxicated and mongering.

We forgot home, our Vessel.

Eyes are tinted and reality lost.

Meaning deferred.

I stood near the window

To myself and looked

Purposeless.

F r a g i l e !

Like silk from the lotus.

Special it is, but who cares?

I still look young.

Am I young?

Or is it the Lotus?

Only Zeus knows.

My Pegasus neighed "It's time."

To dream again the monsters

And acquire the TARGETS.

22/09/2021

31. The Nocturnal

Offered the Chamomile,

Neither calm nor smile.

Nyx[1] was silent and watched,

Her son[2] wandering hith and tith.

He went everywhere but forgot ,

My presence.

I was invisible to him

May be,

Or darker than his Pater[3];

But I saw him flying through noses,

And mouths.

Near to my room I heard my Pater,

Wrapped up like a Wooly Mammoth

Snore the lost Pleistocene.

Selene[4] smiled at my plight,

And the stars blinked with laughter.

Even Wraiths slept under their wreaths,

Waiting their Malaks.

My muse missed her flight I suppose.

She texted her plight.

I looked for connected flights through

Spender, Poe and Neruda.

Sad! They were lost in Auden,

Lenore and Carnal Apples.

Betwixt this, I saw Artemis[5] inducing

An arachnid to weave the silk for a fly.

Hunting of some sort will go on,

On a Starry Night.

Bi, quad, hexa, octa, centi

Or milli pedals,

Mad with desires infamous!

Run with hunger,

Behind something weak.

As I am hunted down,

By million thoughts with wings.

I ran like a madman in search

Of a Muse, a Comrade or even

A Nightingale. None appeared!

Within an infinitesimal,

My routine will come,

From another Zona horaria[6].

Then I will be clicking,

The Lingua Universalis[7]

Till the Rooster's discord.

Dearest Nocturnals,

Kindly send me my Muse,

So that I can fly on Poesy.

OR,

Let Hypnoscome to my lids,

Blackened like Espresso.

Or Selene, prolong your smile,
And shine thy Nyx beautiful.
Let me finish at least a verse,
Or let me sleep like in a hearse.
Incognito!
30/10/2021

32. Amazement

Three ghosts met near a highway.
Usual ones in white and free locks.
A bigger one emerged in front of them
They fist bumped and kept the distance
They thought of a group chat

BIGGER ONE
What was your cause of death?

NECK HUNG
I was dead by hanging

BIGGER ONE
What about you?

BURNT PHIZ
Burnt! As usual.
WET LOCKS
Drowned I was.

BIGGER ONE
I was asking about the real cause.

NECK HUNG
Helpmeet
BURNT PHIZ
The Stock
WET LOCKS
Glitters and Wheels

BIGGER ONE

Oh! Espousal.

NECK HUNG

No, it is the people.

How did you die?

BIGGER ONE

HMMM. I just tried to talk and here I am.

NECK HUNG

What's next for us?

BIGGER ONE

We will be remembered.

The tele will discuss.

Distraction we will be and it will help some.

WET LOCKS

OH! Glorious purpose. ROFL.

Another one came with a fang mark on her legs.

Bigger One added Bitten Legs

BIGGER ONE

What's your story?

BITTEN LEGS

My husband bit me.

BIGGER ONE

Teething?

BITTEN LEGS

The snake it was actually.

But I can't blame it fully.

Venom was his undoubtedly.

NECK HUNG

I think we should kill them all.

BIGGER ONE

No use, some male priest will come to conjure.

And will lock us in his vault as trophies.

Free we are at least now.

WET LOCKS

Is rebirth possible?

BIGGER ONE

Scriptures talk different about it.

Possibility is near to nothing.

BURNT PHIZ

So what is our future?

BIGGER ONE

You can scare some highway smugglers.

Nobody cares who killed them.

People just deem it as accidents.

Or rivalry to some

As it is gold or other intoxicants.

BITTEN LEGS

The same which got us together.

BIGGER ONE

It is a wonderful weapon.

No need to strike with it

Just a thought of it can make you kill

Or get you killed.

Forged it is in the smithies of desire.

Bitten Legs is typing…

WET LOCKS

Will our better halves get punished?

BIGGER ONE

@BITTEN LEGS have a possibility IMAO

BITTEN LEGS

I was about to type that

And @WET LOCKS asked it. LOL.

They waited for the smugglers and trucks

Sadly, it was a day of strike

Against fuel Price hike.

They left cursing patriarchy

And its indispensible anarchy.

Written when a lady was killed in the name of Gold

33. Marijuana

Marijuana,
Yes we are!
The truest form of self
Living in a helix, endless,
Of desires and play
One puff, a journey
Wanderlust! Marijuana,
Never stops at one puff.
It is pursuit after pursuit.
Creates Empires and Worlds
Stays for a second and vanishes.
Limitless fumes enslave him.
Still, he takes another puff.
12/12/2021

34. Stag Party

The booze flew through my Antlers,

I stood with them in the middle of other bucks.

One of the Buck's Nights it was.

We argued and locked our horns like usual.

Rammed the rummies on a pint of rum.

Talked about hinds and their behinds.

Masturbated the *vita irresponsabile*.

Into this, came a Black One uninvited.

It looked at me and exhaled scoff.

Anger anchored on my Antlers!

I charged against it with all my might.

It shattered into a million pieces.

Other ones laughed and I stood anchored..

"You Boozy Buck, you ruined your image!"

Buck grunts of advice from everywhere.

I ran away from there and stood near the Maples.

The Black one was there standing tall,

It came near and poured its hue into mine

I looked at the rivulets and saw my black.

I looked at the party and went back there.

The HERD looked me with suspicion.

As I stood Different and more Antler.

Envious, they called their hounds.

Unheard I stood, Un – herd I became.
Pricey it is! But…
31/12/2021

35. Qalandar am!

Just cleansed my abode
And came back.
Suspended I was,
In that cellular space.
No centre and free to play.
The smell of Vetiver,
Enwrapped the last strand
Of the cob web in some corner.
Spiders and mites stopped,
Their hunt and play,
And greeted their comrade.
I greeted them back.
The water droplets stood,
In pride on my surface.
They magnified the mélange,
Of secrets of my skin.
I told my metal Vitruvian,
To whirl with all might.
The droplets, scared,
Ran away through the alleys,
Of my Metropolis.
Failed and got petrified,
By his windy touch.

I smiled at once
And absorbed them.
We are one now.
The white cirrus towel,
Floated through my Savannah.
Stood I before myself.
In God's image.
I looked at me,
Ecstatic and devoured,
Myself to the lees.
I am more than what I am.
It is asserted every day,
Through my meetings with me.
I am perfect as perfection.
Attires attracted themselves,
Towards my vessel like admirers.
The last button was clipped.
Yes! Enveloped I am in my gears.
It is time for me to wander,
The house of mirrors!
The reflections are imperfect,
They hide my colossal form
With their countenances weak!
They point me as nomad.
Illiterate they are!
I will shatter those illusions,
And emerge shining.

Dancing in ecstasy
Through time and time.
Vagrant, I am without bondage.
To me,
Everything is equal,
As difference should be,
Everything is constant,
As change should be,
Insides and outsides,
Never matter to me.
Intoxicated with Inspiration,
I pass through the three worlds.
01/01/2022

36. The unassailables

If destiny hits you with fire,
You hit back at it as a river.
Flow! With that story to tell.
Again,
As a mountain, it may return,
To disrupt your course.
Fear not! Rise above it
As the blackest cloud,
And burst upon it.
Writ not for an age but a lifetime.

37. Mis Takes

I did a mistake once,
One day,
That same mistake
Opened my door,
And asked, "Can I be
With you always?"
Without waiting for
My answer, it went
To my room.
Now it stays forever!

38. Tomoko in her bath

The vapours of agony rose,
As mercury went upwards.
Furo was camera obscura
Stench métallique,
Enwrapped the bleakness
Gene was there, petrified
Weak and weary he was.
Positioned his third eye
To capture a thought
He thought will fit
For the thoughtless
Aileen escorted the Mater
Ryoko entered hesitant
In her hands lied Tomoko
Beautiful and ready for bath.
Looked him through a corner
Gene's eyes burned and hurt
They were already bluish
Like the waters of Minamata
Thanks to Chisso and Yakuzas.
But it hurts more now
Was it the antiseptic?
Or Tomoko's wrath?

For sneaking around?
He touched his specs
Positioned it along
The bandages and stiches
One touch there, Heaven
Of agony you will see.
Like a Cyclops he looked
And measured the furo
Tomoko lied silent.
Ryoko the excellent
Daughter , chanted a
Song to her intelligent
Daughter. Tomoko smiled.
The only thing she can!
Gene clicked; her eyes too
Clicked. It enquired
"Was it ok?"
It reverberated and spread,
Across Minamata.

NOTES

A Confrontation

1. **Walt Whitman** – American Mystic Poet

2. **The Seven Plagues** – In Revelation 15:1, it says: "Then I saw another sign in heaven, great and marvelous: seven angels having the seven last plagues, for in them the wrath of God is complete." This means that seven angels are given seven bowls of God's wrath, and these bowls are poured out on the wicked and the followers of the Antichrist after the sounding of the seven trumpets.

3. **Sultan** – Vaikom Muhammed Basheer, also known as Beypore Sultan, emphasizes the concept of heterogeneity in his short story "The Inheritors of Earth" (Bhoomiyude Avakaashikal). Basheer reminds us that human beings are not very special and that the Earth is a retreat for all living things, just like it is for humans.

4. **Longinus** - Christian legend has it that Longinus was a blind Roman centurion who thrust the spear into Christ's side at the crucifixion. Some of Jesus's blood fell upon his eyes and he was healed. Upon this miracle Longinus believed in Jesus. ***Godwin, Malcolm (1994). The Holy Grail: Its Origins, Secrets & Meaning Revealed. Viking Penguin. p. 51.***

5. **Because you have seen me, you have believed** – JOHN
   20:29 Jesus said to him, "Thomas, because you have seen Me,
   you have believed. Blessed are those who have not seen and
   yet have believed."

6. **Rest is silence** – HAMLET ACT V SCENE II - *Oh, I'm
   dying, Horatio! This strong poison's overpowering me. I will not
   live to hear the news from England. But I bet Fortinbras will win
   the election to the Danish crown. He's got my vote as I die. So tell
   him that, given the recent events here—oh, the rest is silence. Oh,
   oh, oh, oh. (he dies)* shows the finality.

Aananda Thandav - The Dance of Joy

1. **Shukra -** In Indian mythology, Shukra (which means "bright"
   or "clear") is a sage and an important figure among the Nine
   Planets or Navagrahas. He is considered the spiritual guru of
   the Asura clan. In scientific terms, Shukra refers to the planet
   Venus and is known as both the morning star and the evening
   star.

2. **Himavan –** As per Indian Mythology, Himavan is considered
   as the Lord of the Mountains. Personification of the Himalaya
   Mountain ranges.

3. **Gangotri** – it is a glaciersituated in the district of Uttar Kashi, State of Uttarkhand in Indiaand it is situated on the banks of river Bhagirathi which itself is a source of river Ganga.

4. **Bhagirathi** - An important river in the valley of the Himalyas which is a source river for the river Ganga.

5. **Duns** - In the Garhwali language (spoken in the Uttarakhand region of India), "Dun" or "Doon" refers to a valley situated between the middle Himalayas and the "Shivaliks."

6. **Ringal** – A Variety of Indian Bamboo found in the valleys of the Himalayas

7. **Durga** – A Hindustani Classical Raga which is sang during late evenings. The raga is filled with divine essence and is usually presented for praising deity especially Lord Shiva or Parvathi (Durga)

8. **Indra** – A Vedic God most commonly attributed as the God Thunder, lightning, river storms etc.

9. **Immutable** – In this poem this is regarded as a noun for AUM or Pranava which is perennial and primal sound of the Universe

10. **Kapaala** - a cup made of human skull which is used by mendicants belonging to Shaiva or Buddhist tradition. It is used here as a constant apparatus or vessel where filling and emptying is done symbolizing the universe where creation and destruction occurs which itself is symbolized by Shiva – The God of Eternity.

11. **Third eye** – Shiva's Third eye symbolizes the ultimate consciousness or knowledge. A quality that poets should possess.

The **Muse*** here refers to Parvathi, wife of Lord Shiva. She completes Shiva

The Crown

1. **Marseille** - Marseille, a port city in southern France, has been a crossroads of immigration. It was founded by the Greeks.
2. **Mistral** - strong, cold, northwesterly wind that blows from southern France into the Gulf of Lion in the northern Mediterranean.
3. **Vieux port** – also known as Vieux – Port de Marseille, is an ancient port in France. It is situated in the town of Marseille.
4. **hith and thith** – Hither and Thither just improvised.

Khyber

1. **Khyber** – The Mountain Pass or corridor in the northwest of Pakistan. Well-known migrations of the area have been predominantly through the Khyber Pass.

2. **Citadel** - The Harappan City was divided into the upper town (also called the Citadel) and the lower town. The Citadel assumed the central position of governance and trade.

3. **Sister** – River Saraswati. It is believed that during the later Harappan civilization this river changed its course and dried up triggering a massive drought and eventual decline of the civilization.

4. **Janus** – In ancient Roman religion and myth, Janus is the god of beginnings, gates, transitions, time, duality, doorways, passages, and endings. He is usually depicted as having two faces, since he looks to the future and to the past.

5. **Pastorals –** hereit denotes the shepherds and other tribes who came through the Khyber Pass and assimilated into the Indian subcontinent.

6. **Adam's ale** – Humourous expression for water.

Countenances

1. **Ghent** – A city in Belgium. *The Museum voor Schone Kunsten* (Museum of Fine Arts) is situated here. Many priceless

paintings of old masters are exhibited here.

2. **LENT** – the period preceding Easter, which is devoted to fasting, abstinence, and penitence in commemoration of Christ's fasting in the wilderness. The word "Lent" is derived from the Anglo-Saxon term "lencten" (relating to the lengthening of days), which actually translates to "spring."

3. ***Christus draagt het kruis*** – (Dutch) meaning Christ Carries the Cross. Here it is a painting. The authorship is still a matter of debate.

4. **Jheronimus** – (Dutch) Hieronymus Bosch was a dutch painter and a chief artist of the Early Netherlandish painting school. His paintings are filled with religious allusions.

5. **Visage experimente** – (French) meaning experienced face

6. **Impenitent** – The story of the impenitent thief comes from the New Testament and is about two criminals who were crucified alongside Jesus. In the Gospels of Mark and Matthew, they join the crowd in mocking him, while in the Gospel of Luke, the impenitent thief taunts Jesus about not saving himself.

7. **Joe Blake** – (Australian) snake

8. **Viverrines** – here this term is used for mongoose.

9. **Penitent** – The Penitent Thief, also known as the Good Thief, Grateful Thief, or the Thief on the Cross, is one of two unnamed thieves in Luke's account of the crucifixion of Jesus in the New Testament. According to the Gospel of Luke, he

asked Jesus to "remember him" when Jesus arrived in his kingdom.

10. **One has arrived to wipe a face** – Saint Veronica from Jerusalem encountered Jesus along the Via Dolorosa on the way to Calvary. When she paused to wipe the blood and sweat (Latin sudor) off his face with her veil, his image was imprinted on the cloth. The event is commemorated by the Sixth Station of the Cross.

11. **Holy of Holies** – is a term in the Hebrew Bible which refers to the inner sanctuary of the Tabernacle where God's presence appeared. According to Hebrew Tradition, the area was defined by four pillars which held up the veil of the covering, under which the Ark of the Covenant was held above the floor. The Ark according to Hebrew Scripture contained the Ten Commandments, which were given by God to Moses on Mount Sinai. King Solomon built the Temple in Jerusalem, where the Ark of the Covenant was supposed to be kept.

12. **I see a lineament haggard** – Simon of Cyrene was the man compelled by the Romans to carry the cross of Jesus of Nazareth as Jesus was taken to his crucifixion. This scene is described in Mark 15: 21 – 22, Matthew 27:32 and Luke 23:26 **"And as they came out, they found a man of Cyrene, Simon by name: him they compelled to bear his cross."**

13. **Shiny bald head** – here it denotes Calvary or Golgotha Mount which in hebrew meant 'skull'. In latin Calvary

originated from root Calva which meant either 'skull or bald head'

14. **Empyrean** – The highest part of heaven.

15. **Via Dolorosa** – (Latin) for "Sorrowful Way", often translated "Way of Suffering" is a processional route in the Old City of Jerusalem, believed to be the path that Jesus walked on the way to his crucifixion.

16. **Pelt** – (archaic) it is an act of hurting someone by hurling something towards him/her.

17. **The Man of Sorrows** – This incredible oil painting was created by Robert Campin in the 1430s and is currently on display at the Museum of Fine Arts in Ghent, Belgium. It's also known as the Angels Pietà and has been a popular theme in art since the 14th century. In the painting, the resurrected Christ is seated on the edge of a sarcophagus surrounded by grieving angels, showing his wounds to man. The gold background represents Christ's divinity, symbolizing his immortality and summarizing the entire story of the Birth of Christ in one image. The contrast between the twisted body and expressive rendering of the wounds with the calmness of his face is truly striking!

Safeer - The Man Eater of Nagarhole

1. **Safeer** – (Arabic, Urdu) means Ambassador or mediator.

2. **Nagarhole** – Nagarhole National Park is a national park located in Kodagu district and Mysore district in Karnataka, India. It is one of India's premier Tiger Reserves along with the adjoining Bandipur Tiger Reserve.

3. **Sigur** – The Sigur Plateau (Segur Plateau) is a beautiful plateau in the north and east of the Nilgiri District in the Nilgiri Hills of Tamil Nadu, South India. It covers an area of 778.8 square kilometers (300.7 sq mi) within the Moyar River drainage basin on the northern slopes of the Nilgiri Hills, south of the Moyar River. The incident mentioned in the poem is about the Tiger of Segur, a young man-eating male Bengal tiger that unfortunately killed five people in the Nilgiri Hills of Tamil Nadu, South India. The tiger was eventually taken down by Kenneth Anderson on the banks of the Segur River in 1954.

4. **Gossain** – Gosains, who are also known as Gossains and as Goswami, are Hindu ascetics of India. The term can be translated as master of passion. They are sometimes referred to more generally as Bairagis or Sannyasis.

5. **Anderson** – Kenneth Douglas Stewart Anderson (8 March 1910 30 August 1974) was an India-born, British writer and hunter who wrote books about his adventures in the jungles of South India.

6. **Blue Mountain** – The Nilgiris or nilgiri mountains form part of the Western Ghats in western Tamil Nadu of Southern India.

7. *Tyger Tyger, burning bright* – starting line of the poem, The Tyger. "The Tyger" is a poem by the English poet William Blake published in 1794 as part of the Songs of Experience collection.

8. **Papillae** – The tiger's tongue is covered with numerous small, sharp, rear-facing projections called papillae. These papillae gives the tongue is rough, rasping texture and is designed to help strip feathers, fur and meat from prey.

9. **Santalums** – here it denotes sandalwood.

10. **Kabini** – The Kapila River is one of the major tributaries of the river Cauvery in southern India. It originates in the Wayanad District of Kerala state by the confluence of the Panamaram River and the Mananthavady River. It flows eastward to join the Kaveri River at Tirumakudalu Narasipura in Karnataka.

11. **The ten plagues** – The Plagues of Egypt, in the story of the book of Exodus, are ten disasters inflicted on Egypt by Yahweh, the God of Israel, in order to force the Pharaoh to allow the Israelites to depart from slavery; they serve as "signs and marvels" given by God to answer Pharaoh's taunt that he does not know Yahweh: "The Egyptians shall know that I am the LORD."

12. **Ullal** – Ullal or Uḷḷāla is a City Municipality at Mangalore. It is presently an educational, commercial & industrial hub in Dakshina Kannada district, Karnataka.

13. *Fearful Symmetry* – Fearful Symmetry is a phrase from William Blake's poem "The Tyger" *(Tyger, tyger, burning bright / In the forests of the night, / What immortal hand or eye / Could frame thy fearful symmetry?).*

Rudra Thaandav - The Dance of Destruction

1. **Spiritus Mundi** – (LATIN) here means spirit of the world or simply world.

2. **Neither SI I am nor am I VA – SIVA** - the name as per folk traditions is derived from SI which means "in whom all things lie, pervasiveness" and VA which means "embodiment of grace".

3. **Kapala** – a cup made of human skull which is used by mendicants belonging to Shaiva or Buddhist tradition. It is used here as a constant apparatus or vessel where filling and emptying is done symbolizing the universe where creation and destruction occurs which itself is symbolized by Shiva – The God of Eternity.

4. **Tres Mundos** – (LATIN) three worlds

Heap of the Defile

1. **Muzdalifah** – is an open, level area near Mecca in the Hejazi region of Saudi Arabia that is associated with the Ḥajj ("Pilgrimage"). It lies just southeast of Mina, on the route between Mina and Arafat. After sunset on the ninth day of the Islamic month of Dhūl-Ḥijjah, Muslim pilgrims travel to Muzdalifah, sometimes arriving at night because of overcrowding. After arriving at Muzdalifah, pilgrims pray the Maghrib and ʿIshāʾ prayers jointly, whereas the Isha prayer is shortened to 2 rakats. At Muzdalifah, pilgrims collect pebbles for the Stoning of the Devil (Arabic: Ramī al-Jamarāt, lit. ʿStoning of the Place of Pebbles').
2. **Maghrib** – (sunset prayer) is one of the five mandatory salah (Islamic prayer). As an Islamic day starts at sunset, the Maghrib prayer is technically the first prayer of the day. If counted from midnight, however, it is the fourth prayer of the day.
3. **Isha** – (night prayer) is the night-time daily prayer performed by practicing Muslims. It is the second of the five daily prayers

– (salat). The five daily prayers collectively are one pillar of the Five Pillars of Islam.

4. **Malak -** In Islam, angels (Arabic: malak; plural: malā'ikah) are believed to be celestial beings, created from a luminous origin by Allah. They have different functions, including praising Allah in heavens, interacting with humans ordinary life, and carrying laws of nature.

5. **Nafs –** ego or self.

6. **Iblis -** Iblis is mentioned eleven times in the Quran by name, nine times related to his refusal against God's command to prostrate himself before Adam. The term Shaitan is more prevalent, although Iblis is sometimes referred to as Shaitan; the terms are not interchangeable. The name means remain in grief.

7. **Ibrahim – Abraham.** Islam regards Abraham as a link in the chain of prophets that begins with Adam and culminates in Muhammad. Ibrāhīm is mentioned in 35 chapters of the Quran, more often than any other biblical personage apart from Moses. He is called both a hanif (monotheist) and muslim (one who submits), and Muslims regard him as a prophet and patriarch, the archetype of the perfect Muslim, and the revered reformer of the Kaaba in Mecca. Islamic traditions consider Ibrāhīm (Abraham) the first Pioneer of Islam (which is also called millat Ibrahim, the "religion of Abraham"), and that his purpose and mission throughout his

life was to proclaim the Oneness of God. In Islam, Abraham holds an exalted position among the Major Prophets and he is referred to as "Ibrahim Khalilullah", meaning "Abraham the Beloved of Allah".

8. **Jibrail –Gabriel** (Arabic: Jibrā'īl or Jibrīl in Modern Cairo Edition) is venerated as one of the primary archangels and as the Angel of Revelation in Islam.

Trishanku

1. **Trishanku – Trishanku** (त्रिशंकु) is a king who belonged to Ishvaku descendancy. Trishanku is commonly referred to through mention of "Trishanku's heaven". The word Trishanku has come to denote a middle ground or limbo between one's goals or desires and one's current state or possessions.

2. **Shambhala -** The mythological relevance of the place originates with a prophecy in Vishnu Purana (4.24) according to which Shambhala will be the birthplace of Kalki, the final incarnation of Vishnu, who will usher in a new Age (Satya Yuga).

3. **Limbo** - Limbo (Latin *limbus*, edge or boundary, referring to the edge of Hell) is a postulated viewpoint concerning the afterlife condition of those who die in original sin without being assigned to the Hell of the Damned.

4. **Slow Man** – Title of J.M Coetzee's novel published in 2005 which contains the lines "if you have hitherto been a man, with a man's life, may you henceforth be a dog with a dog's life."

5. **A Right Side** – taken from Franz Kafka's metamorphosis. In that novel, right side is shown as the side of comfort to the protagonist - Gregor Samsa who metamorphosed into a vermin on a fine day. An excerpt from the novel - "Gregor's glance then turned to the window. The dreary weather (the rain drops were falling audibly down on the metal window ledge) made him quite melancholy. 'Why don't I keep sleeping for a little while longer and forget all this foolishness,' he thought. But this was entirely impractical, for he was used to sleeping on his right side, and in his present state he couldn't get himself into this position. No matter how hard he threw himself onto his right side, he always rolled again onto his back. He must have tried it a hundred times, closing his eyes, so that he would not have to see the wriggling legs, and gave up only when he began to feel a light, dull pain in his side which he had never felt before.

6. **Writ in water – John Keats' epitaph - Here lies One Whose Name was *writ in Water*.**

7. **Kafkaesque** - characteristic or reminiscent of the oppressive or nightmarish qualities of Franz Kafka's fictional world.

8. **Samsa or K. –** Characters created by Franz Kafka. Gregor Samsa is the protagonist in The Metmorphosis and Josef K. is the protagonist of The Trial.

9. **Like a hound** - Last words uttered by Josef K. in The Trail.

10. **10. Scylla and Charybdis** - Scylla and Charybdis were mythical sea monsters noted by Homer; Greek mythology sited them on opposite sides of the Strait of Messina between Sicily and Calabria, on the Italian mainland. **Between Scylla and Charybdis** is an idiom deriving from Greek mythology, which has been associated with the proverbial advice "to choose the lesser of two evils".

Alamgir

1. **Alamgir** – The regnal title of Aurangzeb meaning the ruler of world.

2. **The Timurid –** The lineage of Tamerlane or Timur Lang the conquerer. The Mughals were descendants of the Mongol Tribe.

3. **Malak al – Maut –** (Persian/Arabic) The angel of Death.

4. **Muhi – ud – Din -** The real name of Aurangzeb meaning the Reviver of religion.

5. **Takht – e – Taus –** (Persian) The peacock throne.

6. **Bahadur -** (Persian) meaning Brave. On 28 May 1633, Aurangzeb escaped death when a powerful war elephant stampeded through the Mughal Imperial encampment. He rode against the elephant and struck its trunk with a lance, and successfully defended himself from being crushed. His father Shah Jahan provided him the title Bahadur.

7. **Pidargir –** (Persian) meaning he who conquered his own father. Aurangzeb had put Shah Jahan in house arrest and he was always blamed for that.

8. **Was an ornament to the throne -** The name **Aurangzeb** means ornament to the throne.

9. **Gharanas –** In Hindustani music, a gharānā is a system of social organization linking musicians or dancers by lineage or apprenticeship, and by adherence to a particular musical style. A gharana also indicates a comprehensive musicological ideology. This ideology sometimes changes substantially from one gharana to another.

10. **Hadiths –** Hadith means talk or discourse. In Islam, Hadith refers to what Muslims believe to be a record of the words, actions, and, the silent approval of the prophet Muhammad.

11. **Fatawa – Fatawa 'Alamgiri** is a sharia based compilation on statecraft, general ethics, military strategy, economic policy, justice and punishment, that served as the law and principal regulating body of the Mughal Empire during the reign of Aurangzeb Alamgir.

12. **Fiqh** – (Arabic) Islamic Jurisprudence

13. **Uttar and daccan** – North and south – Mughals ruled the north India and during the reign of Aurangzeb, Mughals tried to capture southern India also.

14. **Green and Saffron** – green represent Mughals and saffron represents Marathas. The conflict between Aurangzeb and Maratha Ruler Chathrapathi Sivaji Bhosle is regarded legendary based on the tactics adopted from both the sides. Saffron also resembles the Sikh rebellion that happened during Alamgir's reign especially after the assassination of Guru Tegh Bahadur in 1675. His son, Guru Gobind Singh further militarized Sikhs and created a Sikh Empire after the Khalsa of 1699.

15. **Loo** – A dry wind which blows through the Gangetic plain.

16. **Langar** – is the provision of free food to the needy in a religious context. Its origin is from Sufism (Islam) because serving of food to the needy has been a rich tradition among Sufis, especially of the Chishti Order. This tradition was adopted by Sikhs also.

17. **Rats ate the caps** – Bubonic plague happened during the reign of Aurangzeb

18. **Rasti Rasti** – (Turko – Persian) meaning "In rectitude lies salvation." This was the motto of the Timurid Empire which itself was the descendant of Genghis khan's in Laws or Gurkani

19. **Deepak** – Raag Deepak is one of the six primal ragas of Indian Classical Music. It is believed to be created by Lord Shiva and there is a myth that singing it creates fire.

20. **Malhar** - Malhar is a classical raga. It has the power to create Torrential rains.

21. **Zinda Pir** – (Persian) meaning the living Saint. A title conferred to Aurangzeb.

22. **Badshah Ghazi** – (Persian) meaning the Warrior Emperor

23. **Sikander** – Persian name for Alexander the Great.

24. **Qaiser** – Persian name for Caeser.

25. **Qalam** - Pen

26. **Bhatiyar** – a morning raga which can be sung during the wee hours of morning. This raga has heroic, philosophic and seldom melancholic behavior.

***AZAM** – Aurangzeb's son - **Azam Shah** who ruled the empire after his death but was dethroned and killed by his older half-brother **Prince Shah Alam** later known as **bahadur Shah I.**

Kites of Kabul

1. **Nose** – The pointed front portion of a kite.
2. **Yaar** – Friend or companion.
3. **Tar** – Urdu term for string.
4. **Tapoos** – Pashto term for Kite, a bird of prey.
5. **Kaghazba'd** – Pashto term for paper kite

Sultan

1. **K L Saigal** – Kundan Lal Saigal was an Indian singer – actor who sang the very famous 'So ja Rajkumari' which was one of the beloved songs of the 1940s
2. **Steen** – (here) Mangosteen – a tropical evergreen tree with edible fruit.

The Nocturnal

1. **Nyx** – Greek Goddess of night.
2. **Her Son** – Hypnos, Nyx's son. He is the personification of sleep.

3. **His Pater** – Erebus, Hypnos's father. Personification of darkness.

4. **Selene** – Personification of Moon.

5. **Artemis** – Goddess of hunting and often associated with night and moon.

6. **Zona horaria** – (Spanish) Time Zone.

7. **Lingua Universalis** – (Latin) Universal language. (here English)

71 Haikus

Lost in the forest,

    The tiger introspected,

    "Beware the tricksters!"

The tree mocked a shrub,

"You are weak and die quickly!"

Shrub smiled "Yeah, old one."

Painter drew a street.

The sky put some drops of rain.

Canvas smelled "Complete."

The ghost saw a cake,

His fellow ghost saw the sight,

Said "You died for it."

Cheese smiled at the rat,

The rat smiled back and replied,

"Sorry I saw the trap."

Devil in hell thought,

"Why I was thrown from heaven?

I obeyed myself!"

Tiger said to Lamb

"It's time for me to eat you."

"Be thankful!" said Lamb.

The blind beggar asked,

"Will I find fortune my dear?"

The mute nodded "yes."

Hunter shot a deer,
Birds flew away at the sound,
Tiger smiled at this.

The fly sipped some tea,
"It's sweet! I shall taste again."
Jumped, now tea sips it.

Fish approached the stream,
"Take me to the sea at once!"
Stream said "Know me first!"

Sweet mocked saltiness,
Saltiness replied to sweet
"We both deceive all!"

Heart yelled "March forward!"
Mind whispered "You may fall down."
Body stood still and stared.

Ink dripped from the quill,
Like rain drops from the dark sky,
Poetry sprouted.

Love and hate took race,
Hate won and asked how he won,
Love said "I love you!"

A Ghost asked a Man,
"What you fear the most in life?"
"To become a Ghost!"

Money lender came,
I repaid what he gave me.
I went to the next.

"Precious I am!", Gold,
Medal laughed. Rice grain replied,
"They sell you for me."

Law commanded men.
"Disobey me, you shall rot!"
They served and rotted.

The pond was silent,
Dew dropped its final droplet,
Droplet danced in joy.

With weight of waiting,
I stood near the white window.
Window left, I stood.

I opened a book,
Titled, "Book of Purity."
Ink was white as page.

A wolf saw a sheep,
Sheep greeted the wolf. Wolf yelled
"Hide your fangs, you idiot!"

Early morning asked,
"What is your plan for today?"
I said "rise and set."

Dark blue, grey and black,
Strokes of red, rose and orange,
Dawn it is! Or Dusk?

I ate a mushroom.
Tasteless it was and it said.
"Same as yesterday."

The Black asked the white.
"What makes you superior?"
White said "Your question!"

Autumn commanded,
"Ye Wind, blow out the red leaves!"
Leaves resisted still.

I asked redemption,
"When I am getting redeemed?"
"You were always! But…"

Spider was weaving
A fly flew near it and mocked him
Hard work pays later.

"Like soul from body,
The strings distanced from the self."
Thus spake the Guitar.

Some poured Rioja,
Over sun and clouds muddled.
Sangria red sky.

Gales said to the waves ,
"Ye waves, help me to toss this"
Raft resisted still.

A Pluviophile
Enjoying the petrichor,
Set out on a trip.

Thoughts worse than weeds grew
Through the lawn in my attic
Get me a mower.

I pierced my sharp quill,
Into that snow white paper.
A Murder again.

Vagrant my mind is.
Happy or sad? Befuddled!
Like boat without rows.

Castanets clicked well.
Lobster danced her flamenco.
Net fell, her last act!

A wood walked through men
It saw a nice and tall one.
And etched on his bark.

I enjoyed descent,
Of the Sun through my scotch glass.
Whiskey melted Sun!

Lady Autumn called,
Concierge moon for a night walk.
He became her lamp.

Shriveled myself in,
Agony and blanket. Then,
Heard a hopper leap.

Night was fabulous!
I tattooed myself to the
Moon flower blanket.

The rainbow bubble,
Went to welcome the dark black.
It shattered to death.

My mind wore a mask,
Introspected Vacation
Exhaled and inhaled.

Like an enchanter,
The West wind played its violin.
Dead leaves danced in joy.

Amidst the chaos,
Of the sanity, Insane,
Resorted to peace.

Dynamic! Life is,
Like popcorn in a hot pot.
Loud! It pops and pops.

The tittynopes of,
My last day reminded me,
The spell to survive.

Qalandar am I
A Bird of Passage indeed.
Drifting forever!

Friday the thirteenth,
Today, I met a stranger.
His name was Jason.

Life gave me burgers,
And taught me; "Boy, care all things,
Using both your hands!

The Mountains echoed
The loneliness of the tree
The tree echoed mine.

All I need was love
To rejuvenate and climb
And she gave it well!

Unfathomable!
My love towards her and it,
Beats like rain on leaves.

Evening sky herself,
Mixed peach with frothy white clouds,
And poured it on me.

The dry umbrella
Awaited the arrival
Of another rain.

With his whereabouts,
Kept in place, the satchel waits
Its Master's shoulders.

Purples of Wisdom
Radiate from the Asters
September it is!

The Nimbus looked down,
Upon the city before,
It shot the first drop.

Dearest Choco Shake,
The straw - line space between us,
Sinus invaded!

Dull the mornings may!
But never stop waiting. Your night,
Will come and shine bright.

Sunlight peeped in through,
The Canopies and rested,
On the Verdant floor.

One sleepy morning,
The Sun slowly removed the,
Cloak of mist from trees.

Torchbearer lifted,
Both the torches up above,
People and flies passed.

The Vesper arrived,
Bearing his torch, opening,
The Roseate passage.

The Nature Ordered,
Autumn and waited for it,
With Pumpkin Latte.

In the blue meadows,
Protected by their Shepherd,
The flock of clouds roamed.

Ms. Incandescence,
When I requested to pose,
Flickered with shyness.

Today I stitched my,
Insanity together!
Don't know for how long.

The broken ash tray,
Lamented fumes of glory
And collected dust.

Tomorrow... (an Epilogue)

Reader,

Outside, the Night just descended,

To meet her verdant Earth.

They met and walked through the alleys

And spoke of a better tomorrow.

Tomorrow! I too thought of it

And welcomed the darkness

For the lightful and truthful,

Days to come.

Bye Bye Reader! See you at sometime, somewhere in the

Rumian fields or Basheerian plains, harvesting Words Worthier

than the World itself...

Positively,

Qalandar_am

www.ingramcontent.com/pod-product-compliance
Lightning Source LLC
Chambersburg PA
CBHW020545160726
47991CB00002B/596